Me®

Words of Wisdom

Published by Ron Kaufman Pte Ltd. - 10 9 8 7 6 5 4 3 2

Lift Me Up! - Words of Wisdom
ISBN 981-05-2932-5 - 136 pages.

1. Philosophy
2. Quotations
3. Self-Help
4. Ron Kaufman
5. Title

Cover and page layout by The Bonsey Design Partnership.
Cover illustrations by Ngu Hie Ling.
Set in Times and Arial fonts. Printed in Singapore.

Every effort has been made to credit the original author and make full acknowledgement of the source for each quotation in this text. However, if you know of any instance where the quotation or citation could be more accurate, please send a message to Ron@RonKaufman.com Any corrections will gladly be included in future editions. Thank you.

Below each attributed quotation are **quips, quotes and anecdotes in bold text.** These additional notes are by Ron Kaufman (1956 –), who should be cited as the author in all future works.

Ron Kaufman Pte Ltd
50 Bayshore Park #31-01
Aquamarine Tower
Singapore 469977

Tel: (+65) 6441-2760
Fax: (+65) 6444-8292
Ron@RonKaufman.com
www.RonKaufman.com

Contents

1

Everyday wisdom

Faith in oneself is the best and safest course.

Michelangelo

You are the person living this life. Believe in yourself.

Dream lofty dreams, and as you dream, so shall you become.

James Allen

Know where you are going and the road will appear.

Thought is the original source of all wealth, all success, all material gain, all great discoveries and inventions, and of all achievement.

Claude Bristol

Creative thinking is the source of a creative life.

Big thinking precedes great achievement.

Wilfred Peterson

You want to achieve big things tomorrow? Think big thoughts today!

A man is what he thinks about all day long.

Ralph Waldo Emerson

What do you keep thinking about? That's you!

Every thought is a seed. If you plant crab apples, don't count on harvesting golden delicious.

Bill Meyer

Choose healthy thoughts if you want a healthy harvest.

No problem can stand the assault of sustained thinking.

Voltaire

Catch a problem by the neck and think it to resolution.

The greatest weapon against stress is our ability to choose one thought over another.

William James

Q) What's the greatest stress reliever?
A) Choose relaxing and positive thoughts.

Dissatisfaction and discouragement are not caused by the absence of things but by the absence of vision.

Anonymous

To get from where you are to where you'd rather be, you need a clear idea of where you're going.

If you can't sleep, then get up and do something instead of lying there worrying. It's the worry that gets you, not the lack of sleep.

Dale Carnegie

Action is the only antidote to worry.

Worrying is like a rocking chair, it gives you something to do, but it doesn't get you anywhere.

Ram Dass

Worry doesn't change the facts. Action does.

The palest ink is better than the best memory.

Chinese proverb

Writing down your goals is a big step toward their achievement.

Before you speak, listen. Before you write, think. Before you spend, earn. Before you invest, investigate. Before you criticize, wait. Before you pray, forgive. Before you quit, try. Before you retire, save. Before you die, give.

William Ward

Before you turn the page, read this one again.

People, like nails, lose their effectiveness when they begin to bend.

Walter Landor

Stay focused on your goals and visions.

People don't ask for facts in making up their minds. They would rather have one good, soul-satisfying emotion than a dozen facts.

Robert Leavitt

Sell the feeling.
Sell the sizzle.
Sell the dream.

Great people talk about ideas; average people talk about events; small people talk about other people.

Anonymous

What do you talk about?

When thought becomes excessively painful, action is the finest remedy.

Salman Rushdie

Thinking too hard? Work harder.

Your heart often knows things before your mind does.

Polly Adler

Your feelings are as important as your insights.

Once we realize that imperfect understanding is the human condition there is no shame in being wrong, only in failing to correct our mistakes.

George Soros

The biggest mistake is not to learn from your mistakes.

A desk is a dangerous place from which to view the world.

John le Carré

Get up, get out, walk around.

An intelligence test sometimes shows a person how smart he would have been not to take it.

Laurence Peter

If you score well, that's smart. If you don't, be smart and forget it.

If I have been of service, if I have glimpsed more of the nature and essence of ultimate good, if I am inspired to reach wider horizons of thought and action, if I am at peace with myself, it has been a successful day.

Alex Noble

Before you sleep, ask yourself, 'How was today a successful day?'

Besides the noble art
of getting things done,
there is the noble art of
leaving things undone.
The wisdom of life
consists in the
elimination of non-
essentials.

Lin Yutang

If you are not sure what to do about something, ask youself, 'What will happen if I do nothing about it?'

An idealist believes the
short run doesn't count.
A cynic believes the
long run doesn't matter.
A realist believes that
what is done or left
undone in the short run
determines the long run.

Sydney Harris

What you do today will determine your tomorrow.

There is no use worrying about things over which you have no control, and if you have control, you can do something about them instead of worrying.

Stanley Allyn

Convert your anxiety into action.

You can tell whether a person is clever by his answers. You can tell whether a person is wise by his questions.

Mahfouz Naguib

Listen to questions – yours and others'. The best questions give the most insight and value.

Hard work spotlights the character of people: some turn up their sleeves, some turn up their noses, and some don't turn up at all.

Sam Ewing

Free character test: invitation to work hard.

Laziness may appear attractive, but work gives satisfaction.

Anne Frank

Work focuses the worker and produces the results.

Going to work for a large company is like getting on a train. Are you going sixty miles an hour or is the train going sixty miles an hour and you're just sitting still?

J. Paul Getty

Passengers sit still and watch the world go by. Leaders decide where the train is going.

The ultimate value of life depends upon awareness and the power of contemplation rather than mere survival.

Aristotle

Reflecting upon life deepens your appreciation of life.

Men of genius are admired, men of wealth are envied, men of power are feared; but only men of character are trusted.

Alfred Adler

Be worthy of their trust.

It is only imperfection that complains of what is imperfect. The more perfect we are the more gentle and quiet we become towards the defects of others.

Joseph Addison

The less you focus on others' flaws, the more they see your beauty.

The happiness of your life depends upon the quality of your thoughts: therefore, guard accordingly, and take care that you entertain only notions suitable to virtue and reasonable nature.

Marcus Aurelius

Surround yourself with highest quality thoughts. Discard the rest.

A critic is a man who knows the way but can't drive the car.

Kenneth Tynan

A critic can be helpful for directions. But don't give him the keys to your life.

Anybody can kick down a barn, but it takes a good carpenter to build one.

Sam Rayburn

Being destructive takes effort. Being constructive takes more.

When you want to test the depths of a stream, don't use both feet.

Chinese proverb

What will you do if it's shallow? What will you do if it's deep?

Bright lights cast dark shadows when shone from only one direction.

David Kelly

The world has multiple perspectives. Explore, embrace, enjoy.

Boredom is the feeling that everything is a waste of time; serenity, that nothing is.

Thomas Szasz

With no agenda, no goals, no vision, no aspirations – would you be serene, or bored?

Imagination is the highest kite one can fly.

Lauren Bacall

Soar beyond the clouds of doubt.

The person who has no imagination has no wings.

Muhammad Ali

The person without commitment has no roots.

Imagination is a quality given to a man to compensate him for what he is not, and a sense of humor was provided to console him for what he is.

Oscar Wilde

To live life without imagination is not funny.

A wise man never knows all, only fools know everything.

African proverb

It's wise to know there is much you do not know.

The next best thing to knowing something is knowing where to find it.

Samuel Johnson

www.google.com

Knowledge is power and enthusiasm pulls the switch.

Steve Droke

Knowledge alone is a map. Knowledge with enthusiasm is an adventure.

With so much information now online, it is exceptionally easy to simply dive in and drown.

Alfred Glossbrenner

With information you can drown but not get killed. You can surface, rest, and swim again.

A fanatic is someone who can't change his mind and won't change the subject.

Winston Churchill

...in which case, change who you are talking to.

The optimist proclaims that we live in the best of all possible worlds; and the pessimist fears this is true.

James Cabell

A realist makes the best of the world in which we live.

Optimist: the glass is half full. Pessimist: the glass is half empty. Engineer: the glass is twice as large as it needs to be.

Anonymous

An optimist sees no problem. A pessimist labors the problem. An engineer solves the problem.

When I see a bird that walks like a duck and swims like a duck and quacks like a duck, I call that bird a duck.

Richard Cushing

When all your senses tell you something, pay attention.

Life is the art of drawing sufficient conclusions from insufficient premises.

Samuel Butler

You can't know everything before you choose, but you can know enough to make a choice.

A man is not idle because he is absorbed in thought. There is visible labor and there is invisible labor.

Victor Hugo

Each can be tiring.
Each can be rewarding.

Be vigilant; guard your mind against negative thoughts.

Buddha

Cocoon negatives until they emerge with wings!

The difference between the right word and the almost right word is the difference between lightning and the lightning bug.

Mark Twain

The harvest of old age is the recollection and abundance of blessing previously secured.

Marcus Cicero

My grandfather gave me a thesaurus. At the time I was confused; today I am grateful.

Add to your account whenever you can, draw from it whenever you need.

Make no mistake, my friend: it takes more than money to make men rich.

A.P. Gouthey

Richness is having many things: good health, friends, family, free time, hobbies, work you love...and money.

If you have knowledge, let others light their candles with it.

Margaret Fuller

Warm them with your knowledge. (Don't burn them with your brilliance.)

No man was ever wise by chance.

Lucius Seneca

Wisdom accrues to those who work.

When people go to work, they shouldn't have to leave their hearts at home.

Betty Bender

Heartless work can be heartbreaking. Don't let that happen to yours.

There is a vast world of work out there in this country, where at least 111 million people are employed in this country alone – many of whom are bored out of their minds. All day long.

Richard Bolles

Reach out and *connect* with those around you.

Be regular and orderly in your life, so that you may be violent and original in your work.

Gustave Flaubert

Contain your creativity to create an explosion!

For the sake of getting a living, people forget to live.

Margaret Fuller

Making a living is more than making money.

People who work together will win, whether it be against complex football defenses, or the problems of modern society.

Vince Lombardi

Together we can solve the problems. And we will!

Snowflakes are one of nature's most fragile things, but just look at what they can do when they stick together.

Vesta Kelly

By working together, pooling our resources and building on our strengths, we can accomplish great things.

Ronald Reagan

A snowman is a work of art. An avalanche is a revolution.

The greatest social achievements demand collaboration.

None of us is as smart as all of us.

Japanese proverb

Collective wisdom is always growing.

Don’t wait for people to be friendly, show them how.

Anonymous

Be the one in an elevator who says ‘Good morning!’ to the others.

Keeping score of old scores and scars, getting even and one-upping, always makes you less than you are.

Malcolm Forbes

Let the past be what you left behind.

Kindness is more than deeds. It is an attitude, an expression, a look, a touch. It is anything that lifts another person.

Neil Strait

Serve it up. Pick them up. Lift me up!

Profound wisdom

Man's basic vice, the source of all his evils, is the act of unfocusing his mind; the suspension of his consciousness, which is not blindness, but the refusal to see; not ignorance, but the refusal to know.

Ayn Rand

A leaf under a microscope is a new discovery.

If you keep on doing what you've always done, you'll keep on getting what you've always got.

W.L. Bateman

If you want a change, make a change.

The hours of a wise man are lengthened by his ideas.

Joseph Addison

Live creatively, live longer.

Whatever is at the center of our life will be the source of our security, guidance, wisdom and power.

Stephen Covey

What have you placed at the center of *your* life?

Our finest moments are most likely to occur when we are feeling deeply uncomfortable, unhappy or unfulfilled. For it is only in such moments, propelled by our discomfort, that we are likely to step out of our ruts and start searching for different ways or truer answers.

M. Scott Peck

When your life doesn't feel good, it is a good time to re-examine your life.

Life is a field of unlimited possibilities.

Deepak Chopra

Set sail for something beyond the horizon.

Kindness is more important than wisdom, and the recognition of this is the beginning of wisdom.

Theodore Rubin

Kindness in the beginning, wisdom in the end.

Experience is simply the name we give our mistakes.

Oscar Wilde

More mistakes, more experience. More experience, fewer mistakes.

There was never a genius without a tincture of madness.

Aristotle

Are you kidding?
Are you crazy?
(Are you a genius?)

The sea does not reward those who are too anxious, too greedy, or too impatient. One should lie empty, open, choiceless as a beach – waiting for a gift from the sea.

Anne Morrow Lindberg

Patience is rewarding.

If you are patient in one moment of anger, you will escape a hundred days of sorrow.

Chinese proverb

Angry words can haunt you. Patience never will.

Things do not change; we change.

Henry David Thoreau

If you want to change things, change yourself.

You and I do not see things as they are. We see things as we are.

Anaïs Nin

If you don't like what you are seeing, change what you are being.

Every noble work is at first impossible.

Thomas Carlyle

What is your noble undertaking?

Opportunity comes like a snail, and once past you, it changes into a fleet rabbit and is gone.

Arthur Brisbane

When you see an opportunity you like, grab it.

A person's life is dyed with the color of his imagination.

Marcus Aurelius

Color your life brightly, boldly, beautifully.

Your ‘self’ does not stop where your skin stops; it stops where your imagination stops.

Harry Palmer

If your imagination keeps going, you keep growing.

Not what we have, but what we enjoy, constitutes our abundance.

John Petit-Senn

Enjoy your life completely.

He who is plenteously provided for from within, needs but little from without.

Johann Wolfgang von Goethe

The more you cherish treasure on the inside, the less you'll need to chase it on the outside.

The abundant life does not come to those who have had a lot of obstacles removed from their path by others. It develops from within and is rooted in strong mental and moral fiber.

William Lewis

A chick must crack its own egg to survive beyond the shell.

Abundance is not
something we acquire.
It is something we
tune into.

Wayne Dyer

Abundance is always available – before you, behind you, within you.

The young man knows the rules, but the old man knows the exceptions.

Oliver Wendell Holmes

The best rules are wise guidelines.

In matters of style,
swim with the current;
in matters of principle,
stand like a rock.

Thomas Jefferson

The art of life is knowing when to stand firm and when to swim along.

Restlessness is
discontent – and
discontent is the first
necessity of progress.
Show me a thoroughly
satisfied man and I will
show you a failure.

Thomas Edison

Progress is the path from dissatisfaction to taking action.

Vision is the art of seeing the invisible.

Jonathan Swift

Action is the language of making it visible.

Know the purposes you seek in life, for then, like an archer aiming at a definite mark, you shall more likely attain what you seek.

Aristotle

What is your purpose in this life? Not your goal, nor your dream, nor your objectives – what is your purpose?

Why should we think upon things that are lovely? Because thinking determines life. It is a common habit to blame life upon the environment. Environment modifies life but does not govern life. The soul is stronger than its surroundings.

William James

You think therefore you are. What are you thinking?

In the practice of tolerance, one's enemy is the best teacher.

Dalai Lama

What makes another your enemy reveals more about you than about them.

Man masters nature not by force but by understanding.

Jacob Bronowski

The wind and waves are more powerful than any ship. Don't damn the ocean. Learn to sail!

Thoughts lead to acts, acts lead to habits, habits lead to character – and our character will determine our eternal destiny.

Ezra Benson

Who and how you are today will shape your life tomorrow.

Character builds slowly, but it can be torn down with incredible swiftness.

Faith Baldwin

Every good gesture builds you up. Every lie and meanness tears you down.

Our character is what we do when we think no one is looking.

Jackson Brown

Someone is always watching – you!

It takes a great deal of character to apologize quickly out of one's heart rather than out of pity. A person must have a deep sense of security in fundamental principles and values in order to genuinely apologize.

Stephen Covey

A genuine apology can set things right – and set you free.

There is no fire like passion, there is no shark like hatred, there is no snare like folly, there is no torrent like greed.

Buddha

There is no sunrise like joy, no sunset like affection, no rainbow like love.

Too many wish to be happy before becoming wise.

Susanne Necker

Happiness comes and goes. Wisdom endures.

Before enlightenment: chop wood, carry water. After enlight-enment: chop wood, carry water.

Zen philosophy

Enlightenment is not doing the miraculous. It is seeing the miraculous in what you do.

If you love the sacred and despise the ordinary, you are still bobbing in the ocean of delusion.

Lin-Chi

The ordinary *is* sacred. Look deeper.

A proverb is a short sentence based on long experience.

Miguel de Cervantes

One look can say more than a book.

All I have seen teaches me to trust the creator for all I have not seen.

Ralph Waldo Emerson

The space between the words makes the story. The space between the notes makes the music. The space between your thoughts is your pure being.

Nothing in life is to be feared. It is only to be understood.

Marie Curie

Understanding melts a fear. Understand?

Imagination is the eye of the soul.

Joseph Joubert

Let your soul see clearly, far and wide.

One who has imagination without learning has wings without feet.

Joseph Joubert

The eagle needs a place to stand. Put your ideas to work.

I like to have a thing suggested rather than told in full. When every detail is given, the mind rests satisfied, and the imagination loses the desire to use its own wings.

Thomas Aldrich

We are drowning in information and starving for knowledge.

Roger Rutherford

With eyes, you can see the flower. With your nose you can smell the fragrance. But with your imagination, you can unite with nature.

Information applied gives knowledge. Knowledge applied yields wisdom. Wisdom applied brings success.

Those who stand for nothing fall for anything.

Alexander Hamilton

Take a stand.

In the midst of great joy, do not promise anything. In the midst of great anger, do not answer anyone's letter.

Chinese proverb

To live without regret, act without haste or hatred.

Divisions are imaginary lines drawn by small minds.

Paramahansa Yogananda

Imagine everything unified, connected, one: as it is.

To the man who only has a hammer, everything he encounters begins to look like a nail.

Abraham Maslow

The world we see is a reflection of who we are.

Clay is molded to make a vessel, but the utility of the vessel lies in the space where there is nothing. Thus, taking advantage of what is, we recognize the value of what is not.

Lao-tzu

In companionship, loneliness disappears. By spending time alone, we can become a better companion.

It is never too late to give up your prejudices.

Henry David Thoreau

Better late than never.

Prejudice is the child of ignorance.

William Hazlitt

Complacency is the father.

The ability to quote is a serviceable substitute for wit.

W. Somerset Maugham

Create your own quotation:

'________________________'

Appreciate the person who makes you want to listen when he is with you, and think when he is gone.

Lars Wallentin

Speak to open the minds of others. Listen to open your own.

There are some days I practice positive thinking, and other days I'm not positive I am thinking.

John Eades

If your thoughts are negative, you are not really thinking.

A man is not what he thinks he is, but what he thinks, he is.

Max Hickerson

What do you want to be and become? Think about that!

There is nothing either good or bad, but thinking makes it so.

William Shakespeare

The facts are always neutral. Everything else we add.

The great battle of meditation is with restless thoughts.

Paramahansa Yogananda

To win the battle, rest your mind.

The glow of one warm thought is worth more than money.

Thomas Jefferson

Let your heart be your heater.

One falsehood spoils a thousand truths.

African proverb

Don't lie.

Climb mountains to see the lowlands.

Chinese proverb

Lofty aspirations give you a beautiful perspective on life.

Worry does not empty tomorrow of its sorrow; it empties today of its strength.

Anonymous

Conserve your strength.

I don't know much about creative writing programs. But they're not telling the truth if they don't teach, one, that writing is hard work, and, two, that you have to give up a great deal of life, your pers-onal life, to be a writer.

Doris Lessing

Writing taxes the writer, but it enriches both writer and readers.

When something can be read without effort, great effort has gone into its writing.

Enrique Poncela

When you enjoy the reading, thank the writer.

What I like in a good author isn't what he says, but what he whispers.

Logan Smith

Let a deeper meaning seep between your words.

First, I do not sit down at my desk to put into verse something that is already clear in my mind. If it were clear in my mind, I should have no incentive or need to write about it. We do not write in order to be understood; we write in order to understand.

Robert Day-Lewis

How vain it is to sit down to write when you have not stood up to live.

Henry David Thoreau

When you are not sure about something important, write about it. Your true thoughts and feelings will emerge.

To be bold in your writing, be brave in your living.

Everything you need you already have. You are complete right now, you are a whole, total person, not an apprentice person on the way to someplace else.

Wayne Dyer

Money never made a man happy yet, nor will it. There is nothing in its nature to produce happiness. The more a man has, the more he wants. Instead of filling a vacuum, it makes one.

Benjamin Franklin

No one can be or become you better than you.

Money demands meaning. To have more money, you must create more meaning.

A mind too active is no mind at all.

Theodore Roethke

If you don't focus, you'll spray.

No question is so difficult to answer as that to which the answer is obvious.

George Bernard Shaw

Who are you?
What do you stand for?
Who do you love?

I do not want the peace that passeth from understanding. I want the understanding which bringeth peace.

Helen Keller

I want to know how, but also why.

I want to know how,
but also why.

Wisdom is knowing what to do next; virtue is doing it.

David Jordan

Wisdom without virtue is abstract. Virtue without wisdom is righteous. Wisdom and virtue together are good living.

Never does nature say one thing and wisdom another.

Juvenal

Nature is very wise. Be wise enough to learn from nature.

The more I want to get something done, the less I call it work.

Richard Bach

When something takes me over, I give myself over to it.

What you have outside you counts less than what you have inside you.

B.C. Forbes

The real treasure lies inside you. Bring it out for all to see.

The best way to cheer yourself up is to cheer somebody else up.

Mark Twain

People get turned on by people who *are* turned on. Try it.

The highest destiny of the individual is to serve rather than to rule.

Albert Einstein

How may I serve you?

If things are not going well with you, begin your effort at correcting the situation by carefully examining the service you are rendering, and especially the spirit in which you are rendering it.

Roger Babson

Are you cynical or joyful, resentful or grateful, complacent or committed? What you make of your life is up to you.

All labor that uplifts humanity has dignity and importance and should be undertaken with painstaking excellence.

Martin Luther King, Jr.

Do the best you can.
Be the best you can.

It has always been my belief that a man should do his best, regardless of how much he receives for his services, or the number of people he may be serving, or the class of people served.

Napoleon Hill

Doing something for someone else is reason enough to do it well.

Insightful wisdom

We are shaped and fashioned by what we love.

Johann Wolfgang von Goethe

Love is so powerful, it makes you who you are.

Learning sleeps and snores in libraries, but wisdom is everywhere, wide awake, on tiptoe.

Josh Billings

Don't just read and learn, *live* and learn!

Wisdom is what's left after we've run out of personal opinions.

Cullen Hightower

Personal opinions form and melt away. Wisdom sticks around.

When you know a thing, to hold that you know it; and when you do not know a thing, to allow that you do not know it – this is knowledge.

Confucius

To know there are many things you do not know – this is wisdom.

It is unwise to be too sure of one's own wisdom. It is healthy to be reminded that the strongest might weaken and the wisest might err.

Mohandas Gandhi

The ultimate wisdom is to be open for new wisdom.

Science is organized knowledge. Wisdom is an organized life.

Immanuel Kant

Peace is an organized world.

Knowledge is a process of piling up facts; wisdom lies in their simplification.

Martin Fischer

Genius is in their useful application.

Wisdom consists of the anticipation of consequences.

Norman Cousins

Wisdom comes as we experience the consequences we did not anticipate.

A prudent question is one half of wisdom.

Francis Bacon

Patience to hear the answer is the other.

Common sense in an uncommon degree is what the world calls wisdom.

Samuel Coleridge

Which is why real wisdom is so uncommon.

There is a wisdom of the head, and a wisdom of the heart.

Charles Dickens

Use both.

If facts are the seeds that produce knowledge and wisdom, then the emotions are the fertile soil in which the seeds must grow.

Rachel Carson

Facts without emotions are sterile. Emotions bring facts to life.

Wisdom is the supreme part of happiness.

Sophocles

Serenity is the supreme goal of wisdom.

I feel the degree of a person's intelligence is directly reflected by the number of conflicting attitudes she can bring to bear on the same topic.

Lisa Alther

Different viewpoints let you see the whole.

Only the curious will learn, only the resolute will overcome the obstacles to learning. The quest quotient has always excited me more than the intelligence quotient.

Eugene Wilson

What you want to learn is more interesting than what you already know.

The universe is full of magical things patiently waiting for our wits to grow sharper.

Eden Phillpotts

To sharpen your wits, rest your mind. The universe is patient. You can be, too.

Thoughts have power; thoughts are energy. And you can make your world or break it by your own thinking.

Susan Taylor

Charge your world with positive thoughts. Unleash the power within.

If money is your hope for independence, you will never have it. The only real security that a person will have in this world is a reserve of knowledge, experience and ability.

Henry Ford

You can safeguard your money, but your commitment and capabilities will safeguard you.

The fool doth think he is wise, but the wise man knows himself to be a fool.

William Shakespeare

Don't be so foolish.

It is not white hair that engenders wisdom.

Menander

It's experience that turns your hair white!

Wisdom outweighs any wealth.

Sophocles

Wisdom can generate wealth. Wealth alone cannot make wisdom.

Wisdom doesn't automatically come with old age. Nothing does – except wrinkles. It's true, some wines improve with age. But only if the grapes were good in the first place.

Abigail van Buren

It takes quality of person and quantity of life to yield a brew of wisdom.

The whole problem with the world is that fools and fanatics are always so certain of themselves, but wiser people so full of doubts.

Bertrand Russell

It is wise to pause and consider, but foolish to pause forever. When the time is right, take action.

The older I grow the more I distrust the familiar doctrine that age brings wisdom.

H.L. Mencken

The years bring age. Experience brings wisdom.

The activist is not the man who says the river is dirty. The activist is the man who cleans up the river.

H. Ross Perot

The commentator makes a noise.The activist makes a difference.

Mankind has a great aversion to intellectual labour; but even supposing knowledge to be easily attainable, more people would be content to be ignorant than would take even a little trouble to acquire it.

Samuel Johnson

The little trouble spent acquiring knowledge beats the big trouble of not having it.

Knowledge is power.

Francis Bacon

Sharing knowledge creates even more.

There is only one good, knowledge, and one evil, ignorance.

Socrates

Ignorance is the darkness. Knowledge is the light.

All men by nature desire knowledge.

Aristotle

Which is why children ask so many questions and adults want to know all the answers.

Believe those who are seeking the truth; doubt those who find it.

André Gide

Those who say they have found the truth have stopped looking.

The function of wisdom is to discriminate between good and evil.

Cicero

There are many forms of good, and many forms of evil. Choose wisely.

To know when to be generous and when firm – that is wisdom.

Elbert Hubbard

There are times when being firm is the most generous thing to do.

It is characteristic of wisdom not to do desperate things.

Henry David Thoreau

Bite your tongue.
Hold your horses.
Think again.

Follow your instincts. That's where true wisdom manifests itself.

Oprah Winfrey

That feeling in your gut is well connected.

A short saying often contains much wisdom.

Sophocles

A short saying comes from long reflection.

Turn your wounds into wisdom.

Oprah Winfrey

And the learning itself will heal you.

4

Acquiring wisdom

Wisdom begins in wonder.

Socrates

And ends in indifference.

By three methods we may learn wisdom: first, by reflection, which is noblest; second, by imitation, which is easiest; and third by experience, which is the bitterest.

Confucius

Sometimes it is the bitter medicine that makes you well.

He dares to be a fool, and that is the first step in the direction of wisdom.

James Huneker

The true fool is the one afraid of ever looking like a fool.

The art of being wise is the art of knowing what to overlook.

William James

When you overlook certain things you can focus more clearly on what matters.

Wisdom is the reward you get for a lifetime of listening when you'd have preferred to talk.

Doug Larson

Talking requires another to listen. Who is the wiser?

We don't receive wisdom; we must discover it for ourselves after a journey that no one can take for us or spare us.

Marcel Proust

The journey is your life. Enjoy the ride.

To acquire knowledge, one must study; but to acquire wisdom, one must observe.

Marilyn vos Savant

If you go through life convinced that your way is always best, all the new ideas in the world will pass you by.

Morita Akio

It is not just seeing what happens, but seeing what happens after something happens.

Every new idea begins as a challenge to accepted wisdom.

Let go of your attachment to being right, and suddenly your mind is more open. You're able to benefit from the unique viewpoints of others, without being crippled by your own judgment.

Ralph Marston

Shift your focus from 'I am right' to 'Let me learn from you.'

Minds are like parachutes. They only function when they are open.

James Dewar

An open parachute lets you fly among the clouds and brings you safely back to earth. An open mind does the same.

A closed mind is like a closed book, just a block of wood.

Anonymous

Hence the word for one who will not think: blockhead.

Never mistake knowledge for wisdom. One helps you make a living; the other helps you make a life.

Sandra Carey

Let your wisdom work for you.

Better keep yourself clean and bright. You are the window through which you see the world.

George Bernard Shaw

Clean with your compassion. Scrub with your forgiveness. Rinse with your generosity.

The voyage of discovery is not in seeking new landscapes but in having new eyes.

Marcel Proust

Let go of one prejudice, bias or steadfast conclusion – and your vision will change completely.

The wisdom of the wise and the experience of the ages are perpetuated by quotations.

Benjamin Disraeli

Another good reason for this book!

When I am attacked by gloomy thoughts, nothing helps me so much as running to my books. They quickly absorb me and banish the clouds from my mind.

Savvy Sanders

A good book is good therapy. Cheap, too.

A book is a garden
carried in the pocket.

Chinese proverb

**Enjoy the freshness –
and abundance.**

Those who do not read
are no better off than
those who cannot.

Chinese proverb

Invest in yourself – read!

If you believe every-thing you read, you had better not read.

Japanese proverb

Be able to be alone. Lose not the advantage of solitude.

Thomas Browne

Read what others write to help you think. But think for yourself to decide what you believe.

Many things you see with others. Some things you only realize alone.

When you look for truth outside yourself, it gets farther away.

Anthony Yeo

Search within? Discover. Search outside? Keep searching.

It is not easy to find happiness in ourselves, and it is not possible to find it elsewhere.

Agnes Repplier

When you've decided what you really want, it helps to know where to look.

The first step in wisdom is to question everything – and the last is to come to terms with everything.

George Lichtenberg

Between those two steps is the journey of your life.

The wisest mind has something yet to learn.

George Santayana

And the wisest mind knows it.

The ability to focus attention on important things is a defining characteristic of intelligence.

Robert Shiller

Deciding what's important is just plain smart.

I not only use all the brains that I have, but all that I can borrow.

Woodrow Wilson

Seeking help from others makes you wiser.

Readers are plentiful; thinkers are rare.

Harriet Martineau

Learn to read in school. Learn to think in life.

Do not seek to follow in the footsteps of the wise. Seek what they sought.

Jiddu Krishnamurti

Blaze your own path, for your own life, in your own time.

Good judgment comes from experience, and experience – well, that comes from poor judgment.

Cousin Woodman

When things go right, good for you. When things go wrong, also good for you!

Experience is what you get when you don't get what you want.

Dan Stanford

Later you realize how lucky you were to get exactly what you got.

Remember that not getting what you want is sometimes a wonderful stroke of luck.

Dalai Lama

Disappointed?
Lucky you!

Experience is that marvellous thing that enables you to recognize a mistake when you make it again.

Franklin Jones

Isn't it wonderful to be human?

The man who views the world at fifty the same as he did at twenty has wasted thirty years of his life.

Muhammad Ali

Grow in wisdom as you grow in age.

There are many paths to enlightenment. Be sure to take one with a heart.

Lao-tzu

The path with heart lifts you up even as it tires you out.

What is needed, rather than running away, controlling, suppressing or any other resistance, is understanding fear; that means watch it, learn about it, come directly into contact with it. We are here to learn about fear, not how to escape from it.

Jiddu Krishnamurti

On the other side of fear is freedom. Earn your way to it.

A closed mind is a dying mind.

Edna Ferber

Keep yourself alive!

All human power is a compound of time and patience.

Honoré de Balzac

And effort.

The facts don't need changing at all. The way you see them needs to shift.

Alan Weiss

Facts are just facts. Your point of view gives them meaning.

Seek the wisdom of the ages, but look at the world through the eyes of a child.

Ron Wild

The world was fascinating when you were young. It still is.

What we see depends mainly on what we look for.

John Lubbock

Look for things of beauty and you will see a beautiful world.

Being willing to change allows you to move from a point of view to a viewing point – a higher, more expansive place, from which you can see both sides.

Thomas Crum

When astronauts see the earth from space, everything comes together.

Wise men talk because they have something to say; fools, because they have to say something.

Plato

Speak only when your words improve the silence.

The simplest questions
are most profound.
Where were you born?
Where is your home?
Where are you going?
What are you doing?
Think about these once
in a while and watch
your answers change.

Richard Bach

Life *is* profound. It's that incredible, and simple.

Half of being smart is
knowing what you are
dumb about.

Solomon Short

The other half is finding someone smart about it who can help you.

Wisdom is knowing when to speak your mind and when to mind your speech.

Fernado Flores

The difference between a smart man and a wise man is that a smart man knows what to say, a wise man knows whether or not to say it.

Frank Garafola

It takes courage at times to speak up – and courage at times to shut up.

Some of your wisest moments may be your quietest.

The wise man does at once what the fool does finally.

Baltasar Gracian

When you know it's right, don't debate it. Do it.

The free man is he who does not fear to go to the end of his thought.

Leon Blum

Fulfillment waits at the end.

Rarely do we find men who willingly engage in hard, solid thinking. There is an almost universal quest for easy answers and half-baked solutions. Nothing pains some people more than having to think.

Martin Luther King, Jr.

It's hard work to think hard, but well worth the effort.

Men occasionally stumble on the truth, but most of them pick themselves up and hurry off as if nothing had happened.

Winston Churchill

If you stumble, don't just tumble. Learn something useful from the rumble.

When you are deluded and full of doubt, even a thousand books are not enough. When you have realized understanding, even one word is too much.

Fen-Yang

Insight transcends language.

Not by age but by capacity is wisdom acquired.

Titus Plautus

How full is your life?

A wise man can see more from the bottom of a well than a fool can see from a mountain top.

Leonard Orr

What's seen outside depends on what's inside.

The wise man realizes how little he knows; it is the foolish man who imagines that he knows everything.

Jawaharlal Nehru

Keep looking, keep learning.

Those who wish to appear wise among fools, among the truly wise appear foolish.

Emer Quintilian

Where you play says as much as how you play.

Like an ability or a muscle, hearing your inner wisdom is strengthened by doing it.

Robbie Gass

Your inner voice is speaking. Are you listening?

Men fear thought as they fear nothing else on earth, more than ruin, more than death. Thought is merciless to privilege, established institutions and comfortable habit. Thought looks into the pit of hell and is not afraid. Thought is the light of the world, and the chief glory of man.

Bertrand Russell

Out-of-the-box thinking can be uncomfortable for those who prefer to live in a box.

You can know the name of a bird in all the languages of the world, but when you're finished, you'll know absolutely nothing whatever about the bird. Look at the bird and see what it's doing – that's what counts. I learned very early the difference between knowing the name of something and knowing something.

Richard Feynman

Say 'Happy Birthday'. Now sing it. Got the difference?

The beginning of knowledge is the discovery of something you do not understand.

Frank Herbert

Next is the desire to understand it.

To be conscious that you are ignorant is a great step to knowledge.

Benjamin Disraeli

When you know what you don't know, you have already begun to know it.

There is much pleasure to be gained from useless knowledge.

Bertrand Russell

And pleasure itself is very useful.

Life is the only real counsellor; wisdom unfiltered through personal experience does not become a part of the moral tissue.

Edith Wharton

When you hear something wise, try it out. If it makes sense for you, then you own it.

The quality of our thoughts is bordered on all sides by our facility with language.

Michael Straczynski

Language is a second-order expression of first-order ideas.

I love quotations. It is a joy to find my thoughts beautifully expressed by someone wiser than myself.

Marlene Dietrich

Be wise enough to enjoy the quotes of others, and wild enough to write your own.

The beginning of wisdom is found in doubting; by doubting we come to the question, and by seeking we may come upon the truth.

Pierre Abelard

Seek and find.
Ask and answer.
Doubt and discover.

It is a thousand times better to have common sense without education than to have education without common sense.

Robert Ingersoll

Without common sense,
education is academic.

It's so simple to be wise. Just think of something stupid to say and say the opposite.

Sam Levenson

What would offend someone else? The opposite would likely please them. Try it.

Learn wisdom from the ways of a seedling. A seedling which is never hardened off through stressful situations will never become a strong productive plant.

Stephen Sigmund

Your difficulties are your opportunities to grow stronger.

Good people are good because they've come to wisdom through failure. We get very little wisdom from success, you know.

William Saroyan

Let your failures be your blessings.

He who devotes sixteen hours a day to hard study may become at sixty as wise as he thought himself at twenty.

Mary Little

Accumulating wisdom is a marathon, not a sprint. Keep running, keep learning.

When I can look life in the eyes, grown calm and very coldly wise, life will have given me the truth, and taken in exchange – my youth.

Sara Teasdale

In youth, mistakes. In adulthood, learning. In maturity, appreciation for both.

It requires wisdom to understand wisdom: the music is nothing if the audience is deaf.

Walter Lippmann

Be ready to receive. Listen up.

Thank you for choosing, reading and sharing this book. With 512 positive quotes, notes and anecdotes packed inside, this is one of my favorites:

> Kindness is more important than wisdom, and the recognition of this is the beginning of wisdom.
>
> – Theodore Rubin

Which is your favorite quote? Who will you be kind enough to share it with today?

Wishing you a wise and wonderful life!

To order more copies of the **Lift Me Up!**® books, visit your local bookstore, or www.LiftMeUpBooks.com